in Just-
spring

E. E. Cummings

in Just-spring

paintings by Heidi Goennel

Little, Brown and Company
Boston   Toronto

Also illustrated by Heidi Goennel:

Seasons
When I Grow Up . . .

First Edition

"in Just- ·spring," "hist   wist," and "Tumbling-hair" were
originally published in *Tulips and Chimneys*, E.E.
Cummings's first book of poetry, in 1923.

Library of Congress Cataloging-in-Publication Data
Cummings, E.E. (Edward Estlin), 1894–1962.
    In just- spring.
    Summary: The well-known Cummings poem concerns
the special joys and fears of childhood.
    1. Children's poetry, American. [1. American
poetry] I. Goennel, Heidi, ill. II. Title.
PS3505.U334I5 1987   811'.52   87-14342
ISBN 0-316-16390-2

BP
Published simultaneously in Canada
by Little, Brown & Company (Canada) Limited

Printed in the United States of America

For F.R.S.

—H.G.

I

in Just-
spring   when the world is mud-
luscious the little
lame balloonman

whistles   far   and wee

and eddieandbill come
running from marbles and
piracies and it's
spring

when the world is puddle-wonderful

the queer
old balloonman whistles
far   and   wee
and bettyandisbel come dancing

from hop-scotch and jump-rope and

it's
spring
and

     the

          goat-footed

balloonMan   whistles
far
and
wee

II

hist   whist
little ghostthings
tip-toe
twinkle-toe

little twitchy
witches and tingling
goblins
hob-a-nob   hob-a-nob

little hoppy happy

toad in tweeds

tweeds

little itchy mousies

with scuttling
eyes   rustle and run   and
hidehidehide
whisk

whisk   look out for the old woman
with the wart on her nose
what she'll do to yer
nobody knows

for she knows the devil   ooch
the devil   ouch
the devil
ach   the great

green
dancing
devil
devil

devil
devil

       wheeEEE

III

Tumbling-hair

        picker of buttercups

                violets

dandelions

And the big bullying daisies

through the field wonderful

with eyes a little sorry

Another comes

                       also picking flowers